ABC
REPTILES

ABC REPTILES

Learn the alphabet with reptiles and amphibians!

P.G. Hibbert

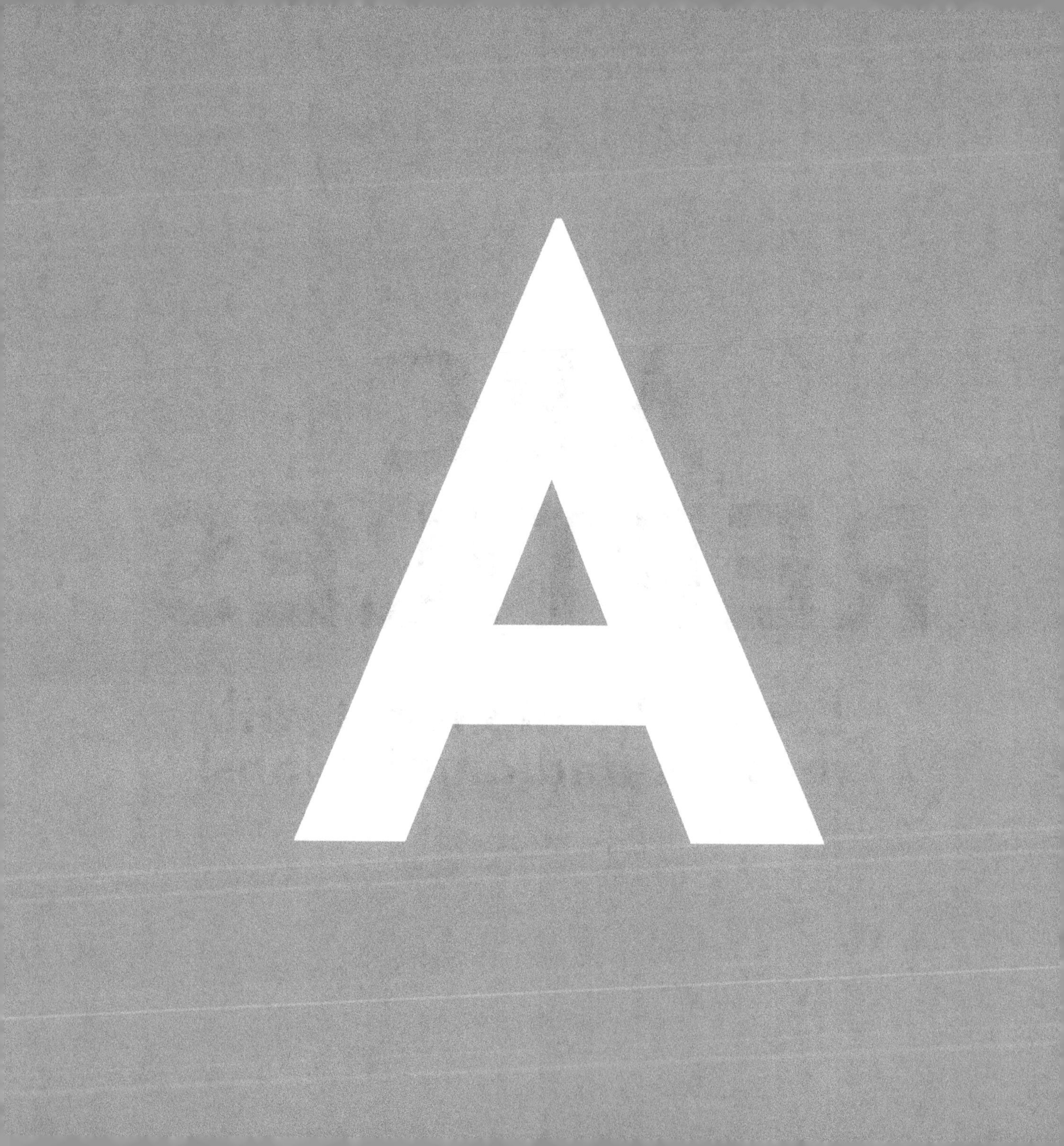

Alligator

Bearded Dragon

Chameleon

Diamondback Western Rattlesnake

Eastern Box
Turtle

Frog

Green Tree Python

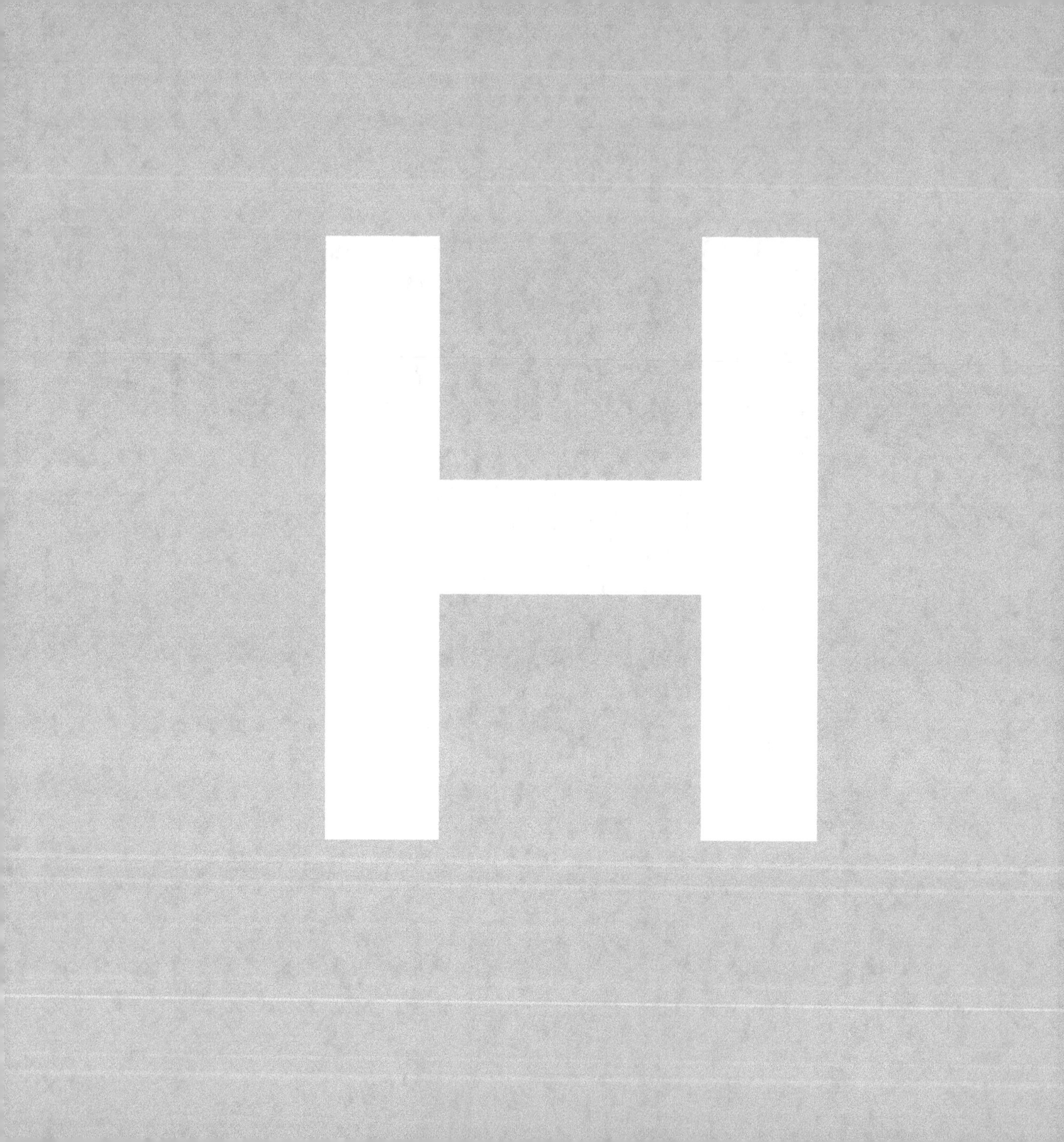

Herptile

Iguana

Johnson's Crocodile

Kaznakow's Viper

Lizard

Monitor

Natural Tree Gecko

Oaxacan Cat-Eyed Snake

Painted terrapin

Queen Snake

Rattlesnake

Snake

Turtle

Uromastyx

V

Variable Coral Snake

Water Moccasin

Xolocalca Bromeliad Salamander

Y

Yellow Gecko

Zambezi
Soft-shelled Turtle

www.ingramcontent.com/pod-product-compliance
Lightning Source LLC
Chambersburg PA
CBHW060233120726
48004CB00012B/1862